TO DO LIST

IN A BOOK

TODOLISTINABOOK.COM

First Edition

TO DO LIST IN A BOOK

- Jet Black -
Cover Design by Go Into Greatness

Go Into
GREATNESS
www.gointogreatness.com

ISBN-13: 978-0998176710
ISBN-10: 0998176710

Printed in the United States of America

THIS BOOK BELONGS TO

_____

TOP 5 TIPS
TO HELP YOU WITH YOUR TO DO LIST & MINDSET

1) PREPARE: To plan your day, we recommend filling out your TO DO LIST the night before.

2) CLARIFY: It's a good idea to start each task on your TO DO LIST with a verb. Be precise! This will help identify the action steps needed to complete each specific task.

3) PROGRESS: Remember, baby steps count. Progress is more important than perfection. It's okay to break down big tasks into something smaller and more manageable.

4) PATIENCE: Sometimes it takes discipline, hard work, consistent effort, and relentless action to succeed at a task or goal. Success doesn't happen overnight. There will be setbacks. Learn from them. Be resilient and keep going.

5) FOCUS: Be fully committed to achieve anything you want. Shut out distractions and pay attention to your priorities. Life is short. Have fun, but most importantly...

Do what matters most.

DATE_____

1 **MUST DO TODAY**
LIST ONE HIGH PRIORITY TASK

○ ☐

2 **SHOULD DO TODAY**
LIST TWO MEDIUM PRIORITY TASKS

○ ☐

○ ☐

3 **COULD DO TODAY**
LIST THREE LOW PRIORITY TASKS

○ ☐

○ ☐

○ ☐

1 **MUST DO TODAY**
LIST ONE HIGH PRIORITY TASK

○ ☐

2 **SHOULD DO TODAY**
LIST TWO MEDIUM PRIORITY TASKS

○ ☐

○ ☐

3 **COULD DO TODAY**
LIST THREE LOW PRIORITY TASKS

○ ☐

○ ☐

○ ☐

DATE_____

1 **MUST DO TODAY**
LIST ONE HIGH PRIORITY TASK

- ☐

2 **SHOULD DO TODAY**
LIST TWO MEDIUM PRIORITY TASKS

- ☐

- ☐

3 **COULD DO TODAY**
LIST THREE LOW PRIORITY TASKS

- ☐
- ☐
- ☐

1 **MUST DO TODAY**
LIST ONE HIGH PRIORITY TASK

○ ☐

2 **SHOULD DO TODAY**
LIST TWO MEDIUM PRIORITY TASKS

○ ☐

○ ☐

3 **COULD DO TODAY**
LIST THREE LOW PRIORITY TASKS

○ ☐

○ ☐

○ ☐

1 MUST DO TODAY
LIST ONE HIGH PRIORITY TASK

○ ☐

2 SHOULD DO TODAY
LIST TWO MEDIUM PRIORITY TASKS

○ ☐

○ ☐

3 COULD DO TODAY
LIST THREE LOW PRIORITY TASKS

○ ☐

○ ☐

○ ☐

1 **MUST DO TODAY**
LIST ONE HIGH PRIORITY TASK

○   ☐

2 **SHOULD DO TODAY**
LIST TWO MEDIUM PRIORITY TASKS

○   ☐

○   ☐

3 **COULD DO TODAY**
LIST THREE LOW PRIORITY TASKS

○   ☐

○   ☐

○   ☐

1 **MUST DO TODAY**
LIST ONE HIGH PRIORITY TASK

○ ☐

2 **SHOULD DO TODAY**
LIST TWO MEDIUM PRIORITY TASKS

○ ☐

○ ☐

3 **COULD DO TODAY**
LIST THREE LOW PRIORITY TASKS

○ ☐

○ ☐

○ ☐

1 **MUST DO TODAY**
LIST ONE HIGH PRIORITY TASK

○ ☐

2 **SHOULD DO TODAY**
LIST TWO MEDIUM PRIORITY TASKS

○ ☐

○ ☐

3 **COULD DO TODAY**
LIST THREE LOW PRIORITY TASKS

○ ☐

○ ☐

○ ☐

1 **MUST DO TODAY**
LIST ONE HIGH PRIORITY TASK

○

☐

2 **SHOULD DO TODAY**
LIST TWO MEDIUM PRIORITY TASKS

○

☐

○

☐

3 **COULD DO TODAY**
LIST THREE LOW PRIORITY TASKS

○   ☐

○   ☐

○   ☐

1 **MUST DO TODAY**
LIST ONE HIGH PRIORITY TASK

○ ☐

2 **SHOULD DO TODAY**
LIST TWO MEDIUM PRIORITY TASKS

○ ☐

○ ☐

3 **COULD DO TODAY**
LIST THREE LOW PRIORITY TASKS

○ ☐

○ ☐

○ ☐

1 MUST DO TODAY
LIST ONE HIGH PRIORITY TASK

○

☐

2 SHOULD DO TODAY
LIST TWO MEDIUM PRIORITY TASKS

○

☐

○

☐

3 COULD DO TODAY
LIST THREE LOW PRIORITY TASKS

○ ☐

○ ☐

○ ☐

1 **MUST DO TODAY**
LIST ONE HIGH PRIORITY TASK

○

2 **SHOULD DO TODAY**
LIST TWO MEDIUM PRIORITY TASKS

○

○

3 **COULD DO TODAY**
LIST THREE LOW PRIORITY TASKS

○

○

○

1 MUST DO TODAY
LIST ONE HIGH PRIORITY TASK

○

☐

2 SHOULD DO TODAY
LIST TWO MEDIUM PRIORITY TASKS

○

☐

○

☐

3 COULD DO TODAY
LIST THREE LOW PRIORITY TASKS

○   ☐

○   ☐

○   ☐

1 MUST DO TODAY
LIST ONE HIGH PRIORITY TASK

○   ☐

2 SHOULD DO TODAY
LIST TWO MEDIUM PRIORITY TASKS

○   ☐

○   ☐

3 COULD DO TODAY
LIST THREE LOW PRIORITY TASKS

○   ☐

○   ☐

○   ☐

1 **MUST DO TODAY**
LIST ONE HIGH PRIORITY TASK

○

☐

2 **SHOULD DO TODAY**
LIST TWO MEDIUM PRIORITY TASKS

○

☐

○

☐

3 **COULD DO TODAY**
LIST THREE LOW PRIORITY TASKS

○ ☐

○ ☐

○ ☐

1 **MUST DO TODAY**
LIST ONE HIGH PRIORITY TASK

○   ☐

2 **SHOULD DO TODAY**
LIST TWO MEDIUM PRIORITY TASKS

○   ☐

○   ☐

3 **COULD DO TODAY**
LIST THREE LOW PRIORITY TASKS

○   ☐

○   ☐

○   ☐

DATE_____

1 MUST DO TODAY
LIST ONE HIGH PRIORITY TASK

○ ☐

2 SHOULD DO TODAY
LIST TWO MEDIUM PRIORITY TASKS

○ ☐

○ ☐

3 COULD DO TODAY
LIST THREE LOW PRIORITY TASKS

○ ☐

○ ☐

○ ☐

1 MUST DO TODAY
LIST ONE HIGH PRIORITY TASK

○ ☐

2 SHOULD DO TODAY
LIST TWO MEDIUM PRIORITY TASKS

○ ☐

○ ☐

3 COULD DO TODAY
LIST THREE LOW PRIORITY TASKS

○ ☐

○ ☐

○ ☐

1 **MUST DO TODAY**
LIST ONE HIGH PRIORITY TASK

○

☐

2 **SHOULD DO TODAY**
LIST TWO MEDIUM PRIORITY TASKS

○

☐

○

☐

3 **COULD DO TODAY**
LIST THREE LOW PRIORITY TASKS

○   ☐

○   ☐

○   ☐

1 | MUST DO TODAY
LIST ONE HIGH PRIORITY TASK

○ ☐

2 | SHOULD DO TODAY
LIST TWO MEDIUM PRIORITY TASKS

○ ☐

○ ☐

3 | COULD DO TODAY
LIST THREE LOW PRIORITY TASKS

○ ☐

○ ☐

○ ☐

1 **MUST DO TODAY**
LIST ONE HIGH PRIORITY TASK

○

2 **SHOULD DO TODAY**
LIST TWO MEDIUM PRIORITY TASKS

○

○

3 **COULD DO TODAY**
LIST THREE LOW PRIORITY TASKS

○

○

○

1 **MUST DO TODAY**
LIST ONE HIGH PRIORITY TASK

○

☐

2 **SHOULD DO TODAY**
LIST TWO MEDIUM PRIORITY TASKS

○

☐

○

☐

3 **COULD DO TODAY**
LIST THREE LOW PRIORITY TASKS

○   ☐

○   ☐

○   ☐

DATE_____

1 **MUST DO TODAY**
LIST ONE HIGH PRIORITY TASK

○ ☐

2 **SHOULD DO TODAY**
LIST TWO MEDIUM PRIORITY TASKS

○ ☐

○ ☐

3 **COULD DO TODAY**
LIST THREE LOW PRIORITY TASKS

○ ☐

○ ☐

○ ☐

1 **MUST DO TODAY**
LIST ONE HIGH PRIORITY TASK

○ ☐

2 **SHOULD DO TODAY**
LIST TWO MEDIUM PRIORITY TASKS

○ ☐

○ ☐

3 **COULD DO TODAY**
LIST THREE LOW PRIORITY TASKS

○ ☐

○ ☐

○ ☐

DATE_____

1 **MUST DO TODAY**
LIST ONE HIGH PRIORITY TASK

○ ☐

2 **SHOULD DO TODAY**
LIST TWO MEDIUM PRIORITY TASKS

○ ☐

○ ☐

3 **COULD DO TODAY**
LIST THREE LOW PRIORITY TASKS

○ ☐

○ ☐

○ ☐

DATE_____

1 MUST DO TODAY
LIST ONE HIGH PRIORITY TASK

○ ☐

2 SHOULD DO TODAY
LIST TWO MEDIUM PRIORITY TASKS

○ ☐

○ ☐

3 COULD DO TODAY
LIST THREE LOW PRIORITY TASKS

○ ☐

○ ☐

○ ☐

DATE_____

1 **MUST DO TODAY**
LIST ONE HIGH PRIORITY TASK

○   ☐

2 **SHOULD DO TODAY**
LIST TWO MEDIUM PRIORITY TASKS

○   ☐

○   ☐

3 **COULD DO TODAY**
LIST THREE LOW PRIORITY TASKS

○   ☐

○   ☐

○   ☐

1 **MUST DO TODAY**
LIST ONE HIGH PRIORITY TASK

○

☐

2 **SHOULD DO TODAY**
LIST TWO MEDIUM PRIORITY TASKS

○

☐

○

☐

3 **COULD DO TODAY**
LIST THREE LOW PRIORITY TASKS

○ ☐

○ ☐

○ ☐

1 **MUST DO TODAY**
LIST ONE HIGH PRIORITY TASK

○   ☐

2 **SHOULD DO TODAY**
LIST TWO MEDIUM PRIORITY TASKS

○   ☐

○   ☐

3 **COULD DO TODAY**
LIST THREE LOW PRIORITY TASKS

○   ☐

○   ☐

○   ☐

1 MUST DO TODAY
LIST ONE HIGH PRIORITY TASK

○ ☐

2 SHOULD DO TODAY
LIST TWO MEDIUM PRIORITY TASKS

○ ☐

○ ☐

3 COULD DO TODAY
LIST THREE LOW PRIORITY TASKS

○ ☐

○ ☐

○ ☐

1 **MUST DO TODAY**
LIST ONE HIGH PRIORITY TASK

○ ☐

2 **SHOULD DO TODAY**
LIST TWO MEDIUM PRIORITY TASKS

○ ☐

○ ☐

3 **COULD DO TODAY**
LIST THREE LOW PRIORITY TASKS

○ ☐

○ ☐

○ ☐

1 MUST DO TODAY
LIST ONE HIGH PRIORITY TASK

○ ☐

2 SHOULD DO TODAY
LIST TWO MEDIUM PRIORITY TASKS

○ ☐

○ ☐

3 COULD DO TODAY
LIST THREE LOW PRIORITY TASKS

○ ☐

○ ☐

○ ☐

DATE_____

1 MUST DO TODAY
LIST ONE HIGH PRIORITY TASK

○

☐

2 SHOULD DO TODAY
LIST TWO MEDIUM PRIORITY TASKS

○

☐

○

☐

3 COULD DO TODAY
LIST THREE LOW PRIORITY TASKS

○   ☐

○   ☐

○   ☐

1 **MUST DO TODAY**
LIST ONE HIGH PRIORITY TASK

○   ☐

2 **SHOULD DO TODAY**
LIST TWO MEDIUM PRIORITY TASKS

○   ☐

○   ☐

3 **COULD DO TODAY**
LIST THREE LOW PRIORITY TASKS

○   ☐

○   ☐

○   ☐

1 **MUST DO TODAY**
LIST ONE HIGH PRIORITY TASK

○ ☐

2 **SHOULD DO TODAY**
LIST TWO MEDIUM PRIORITY TASKS

○ ☐

○ ☐

3 **COULD DO TODAY**
LIST THREE LOW PRIORITY TASKS

○ ☐

○ ☐

○ ☐

1 **MUST DO TODAY**
LIST ONE HIGH PRIORITY TASK

○ ☐

2 **SHOULD DO TODAY**
LIST TWO MEDIUM PRIORITY TASKS

○ ☐

○ ☐

3 **COULD DO TODAY**
LIST THREE LOW PRIORITY TASKS

○ ☐

○ ☐

○ ☐

1 MUST DO TODAY
LIST ONE HIGH PRIORITY TASK

○

☐

2 SHOULD DO TODAY
LIST TWO MEDIUM PRIORITY TASKS

○

☐

○

☐

3 COULD DO TODAY
LIST THREE LOW PRIORITY TASKS

○ ☐

○ ☐

○ ☐

1 MUST DO TODAY
LIST ONE HIGH PRIORITY TASK

○ ☐

2 SHOULD DO TODAY
LIST TWO MEDIUM PRIORITY TASKS

○ ☐

○ ☐

3 COULD DO TODAY
LIST THREE LOW PRIORITY TASKS

○ ☐

○ ☐

○ ☐

1 **MUST DO TODAY**
LIST ONE HIGH PRIORITY TASK

○ ☐

2 **SHOULD DO TODAY**
LIST TWO MEDIUM PRIORITY TASKS

○ ☐

○ ☐

3 **COULD DO TODAY**
LIST THREE LOW PRIORITY TASKS

○ ☐

○ ☐

○ ☐

1 **MUST DO TODAY**
LIST ONE HIGH PRIORITY TASK

○

☐

2 **SHOULD DO TODAY**
LIST TWO MEDIUM PRIORITY TASKS

○

☐

○

☐

3 **COULD DO TODAY**
LIST THREE LOW PRIORITY TASKS

○   ☐

○   ☐

○   ☐

1 **MUST DO TODAY**
LIST ONE HIGH PRIORITY TASK

○

2 **SHOULD DO TODAY**
LIST TWO MEDIUM PRIORITY TASKS

○

○

3 **COULD DO TODAY**
LIST THREE LOW PRIORITY TASKS

○

○

○

1 **MUST DO TODAY**
LIST ONE HIGH PRIORITY TASK

○

☐

2 **SHOULD DO TODAY**
LIST TWO MEDIUM PRIORITY TASKS

○

☐

○

☐

3 **COULD DO TODAY**
LIST THREE LOW PRIORITY TASKS

○   ☐

○   ☐

○   ☐

1 **MUST DO TODAY**
LIST ONE HIGH PRIORITY TASK

○
☐

2 **SHOULD DO TODAY**
LIST TWO MEDIUM PRIORITY TASKS

○
☐

○
☐

3 **COULD DO TODAY**
LIST THREE LOW PRIORITY TASKS

○
☐

○
☐

○
☐

1 **MUST DO TODAY**
LIST ONE HIGH PRIORITY TASK

○ ☐

2 **SHOULD DO TODAY**
LIST TWO MEDIUM PRIORITY TASKS

○ ☐

○ ☐

3 **COULD DO TODAY**
LIST THREE LOW PRIORITY TASKS

○ ☐

○ ☐

○ ☐

1 **MUST DO TODAY**
LIST ONE HIGH PRIORITY TASK

○   ☐

2 **SHOULD DO TODAY**
LIST TWO MEDIUM PRIORITY TASKS

○   ☐

○   ☐

3 **COULD DO TODAY**
LIST THREE LOW PRIORITY TASKS

○   ☐

○   ☐

○   ☐

1 **MUST DO TODAY**
LIST ONE HIGH PRIORITY TASK

○

☐

2 **SHOULD DO TODAY**
LIST TWO MEDIUM PRIORITY TASKS

○

☐

○

☐

3 **COULD DO TODAY**
LIST THREE LOW PRIORITY TASKS

○   ☐

○   ☐

○   ☐

1 **MUST DO TODAY**
LIST ONE HIGH PRIORITY TASK

○ ☐

2 **SHOULD DO TODAY**
LIST TWO MEDIUM PRIORITY TASKS

○ ☐

○ ☐

3 **COULD DO TODAY**
LIST THREE LOW PRIORITY TASKS

○ ☐

○ ☐

○ ☐

DATE_____

1 **MUST DO TODAY**
LIST ONE HIGH PRIORITY TASK

○   ☐

2 **SHOULD DO TODAY**
LIST TWO MEDIUM PRIORITY TASKS

○   ☐

○   ☐

3 **COULD DO TODAY**
LIST THREE LOW PRIORITY TASKS

○   ☐

○   ☐

○   ☐

48

1 MUST DO TODAY
LIST ONE HIGH PRIORITY TASK

○

☐

2 SHOULD DO TODAY
LIST TWO MEDIUM PRIORITY TASKS

○

☐

○

☐

3 COULD DO TODAY
LIST THREE LOW PRIORITY TASKS

○ ☐

○ ☐

○ ☐

1 **MUST DO TODAY**
LIST ONE HIGH PRIORITY TASK

○ ☐

2 **SHOULD DO TODAY**
LIST TWO MEDIUM PRIORITY TASKS

○ ☐

○ ☐

3 **COULD DO TODAY**
LIST THREE LOW PRIORITY TASKS

○ ☐

○ ☐

○ ☐

1 MUST DO TODAY
LIST ONE HIGH PRIORITY TASK

○

□

2 SHOULD DO TODAY
LIST TWO MEDIUM PRIORITY TASKS

○

□

○

□

3 COULD DO TODAY
LIST THREE LOW PRIORITY TASKS

○   □

○   □

○   □

DATE_____

1 **MUST DO TODAY**
LIST ONE HIGH PRIORITY TASK

○ ☐

2 **SHOULD DO TODAY**
LIST TWO MEDIUM PRIORITY TASKS

○ ☐

○ ☐

3 **COULD DO TODAY**
LIST THREE LOW PRIORITY TASKS

○ ☐

○ ☐

○ ☐

1 MUST DO TODAY
LIST ONE HIGH PRIORITY TASK

○   ☐

2 SHOULD DO TODAY
LIST TWO MEDIUM PRIORITY TASKS

○   ☐

○   ☐

3 COULD DO TODAY
LIST THREE LOW PRIORITY TASKS

○   ☐

○   ☐

○   ☐

1 **MUST DO TODAY**
LIST ONE HIGH PRIORITY TASK

○   ☐

2 **SHOULD DO TODAY**
LIST TWO MEDIUM PRIORITY TASKS

○   ☐

○   ☐

3 **COULD DO TODAY**
LIST THREE LOW PRIORITY TASKS

○   ☐

○   ☐

○   ☐

1 **MUST DO TODAY**
LIST ONE HIGH PRIORITY TASK

○   ☐

2 **SHOULD DO TODAY**
LIST TWO MEDIUM PRIORITY TASKS

○   ☐

○   ☐

3 **COULD DO TODAY**
LIST THREE LOW PRIORITY TASKS

○   ☐

○   ☐

○   ☐

1 **MUST DO TODAY**
LIST ONE HIGH PRIORITY TASK

○ ☐

2 **SHOULD DO TODAY**
LIST TWO MEDIUM PRIORITY TASKS

○ ☐

○ ☐

3 **COULD DO TODAY**
LIST THREE LOW PRIORITY TASKS

○ ☐

○ ☐

○ ☐

1 MUST DO TODAY
LIST ONE HIGH PRIORITY TASK

○ ☐

2 SHOULD DO TODAY
LIST TWO MEDIUM PRIORITY TASKS

○ ☐

○ ☐

3 COULD DO TODAY
LIST THREE LOW PRIORITY TASKS

○ ☐

○ ☐

○ ☐

1 **MUST DO TODAY**
LIST ONE HIGH PRIORITY TASK

○

☐

2 **SHOULD DO TODAY**
LIST TWO MEDIUM PRIORITY TASKS

○

☐

○

☐

3 **COULD DO TODAY**
LIST THREE LOW PRIORITY TASKS

○ ☐

○ ☐

○ ☐

1 **MUST DO TODAY**
LIST ONE HIGH PRIORITY TASK

○   ☐

2 **SHOULD DO TODAY**
LIST TWO MEDIUM PRIORITY TASKS

○   ☐

○   ☐

3 **COULD DO TODAY**
LIST THREE LOW PRIORITY TASKS

○   ☐

○   ☐

○   ☐

1 **MUST DO TODAY**
LIST ONE HIGH PRIORITY TASK

○   ☐

2 **SHOULD DO TODAY**
LIST TWO MEDIUM PRIORITY TASKS

○   ☐

○   ☐

3 **COULD DO TODAY**
LIST THREE LOW PRIORITY TASKS

○   ☐

○   ☐

○   ☐

1 MUST DO TODAY
LIST ONE HIGH PRIORITY TASK

○ ☐

2 SHOULD DO TODAY
LIST TWO MEDIUM PRIORITY TASKS

○ ☐

○ ☐

3 COULD DO TODAY
LIST THREE LOW PRIORITY TASKS

○ ☐

○ ☐

○ ☐

1 **MUST DO TODAY**
LIST ONE HIGH PRIORITY TASK

2 **SHOULD DO TODAY**
LIST TWO MEDIUM PRIORITY TASKS

3 **COULD DO TODAY**
LIST THREE LOW PRIORITY TASKS

1 **MUST DO TODAY**
LIST ONE HIGH PRIORITY TASK

○
☐

2 **SHOULD DO TODAY**
LIST TWO MEDIUM PRIORITY TASKS

○
☐

○
☐

3 **COULD DO TODAY**
LIST THREE LOW PRIORITY TASKS

○ ☐

○ ☐

○ ☐

DATE_____

1 MUST DO TODAY
LIST ONE HIGH PRIORITY TASK

○ ☐

2 SHOULD DO TODAY
LIST TWO MEDIUM PRIORITY TASKS

○ ☐

○ ☐

3 COULD DO TODAY
LIST THREE LOW PRIORITY TASKS

○ ☐

○ ☐

○ ☐

1 MUST DO TODAY
LIST ONE HIGH PRIORITY TASK

○

☐

2 SHOULD DO TODAY
LIST TWO MEDIUM PRIORITY TASKS

○

☐

○

☐

3 COULD DO TODAY
LIST THREE LOW PRIORITY TASKS

○ ☐

○ ☐

○ ☐

1 **MUST DO TODAY**
LIST ONE HIGH PRIORITY TASK

○

☐

2 **SHOULD DO TODAY**
LIST TWO MEDIUM PRIORITY TASKS

○

☐

○

☐

3 **COULD DO TODAY**
LIST THREE LOW PRIORITY TASKS

○   ☐

○   ☐

○   ☐

1 MUST DO TODAY
LIST ONE HIGH PRIORITY TASK

○   ☐

2 SHOULD DO TODAY
LIST TWO MEDIUM PRIORITY TASKS

○   ☐

○   ☐

3 COULD DO TODAY
LIST THREE LOW PRIORITY TASKS

○   ☐

○   ☐

○   ☐

1 **MUST DO TODAY**
LIST ONE HIGH PRIORITY TASK

○

2 **SHOULD DO TODAY**
LIST TWO MEDIUM PRIORITY TASKS

○

○

3 **COULD DO TODAY**
LIST THREE LOW PRIORITY TASKS

○

○

○

1 **MUST DO TODAY**
LIST ONE HIGH PRIORITY TASK

○ ☐

2 **SHOULD DO TODAY**
LIST TWO MEDIUM PRIORITY TASKS

○ ☐

○ ☐

3 **COULD DO TODAY**
LIST THREE LOW PRIORITY TASKS

○ ☐

○ ☐

○ ☐

1 MUST DO TODAY
LIST ONE HIGH PRIORITY TASK

○ ☐

2 SHOULD DO TODAY
LIST TWO MEDIUM PRIORITY TASKS

○ ☐

○ ☐

3 COULD DO TODAY
LIST THREE LOW PRIORITY TASKS

○ ☐

○ ☐

○ ☐

1 **MUST DO TODAY**
LIST ONE HIGH PRIORITY TASK

○

▢

2 **SHOULD DO TODAY**
LIST TWO MEDIUM PRIORITY TASKS

○

▢

○

▢

3 **COULD DO TODAY**
LIST THREE LOW PRIORITY TASKS

○   ▢

○   ▢

○   ▢

1 **MUST DO TODAY**
LIST ONE HIGH PRIORITY TASK

○ ☐

2 **SHOULD DO TODAY**
LIST TWO MEDIUM PRIORITY TASKS

○ ☐

○ ☐

3 **COULD DO TODAY**
LIST THREE LOW PRIORITY TASKS

○ ☐

○ ☐

○ ☐

1 **MUST DO TODAY**
LIST ONE HIGH PRIORITY TASK

○

☐

2 **SHOULD DO TODAY**
LIST TWO MEDIUM PRIORITY TASKS

○

☐

○

☐

3 **COULD DO TODAY**
LIST THREE LOW PRIORITY TASKS

○   ☐

○   ☐

○   ☐

1 **MUST DO TODAY**
LIST ONE HIGH PRIORITY TASK

○ ☐

2 **SHOULD DO TODAY**
LIST TWO MEDIUM PRIORITY TASKS

○ ☐

○ ☐

3 **COULD DO TODAY**
LIST THREE LOW PRIORITY TASKS

○ ☐

○ ☐

○ ☐

DATE_____

1 MUST DO TODAY
LIST ONE HIGH PRIORITY TASK

○   ☐

2 SHOULD DO TODAY
LIST TWO MEDIUM PRIORITY TASKS

○   ☐

○   ☐

3 COULD DO TODAY
LIST THREE LOW PRIORITY TASKS

○   ☐

○   ☐

○   ☐

1 MUST DO TODAY
LIST ONE HIGH PRIORITY TASK

○ ☐

2 SHOULD DO TODAY
LIST TWO MEDIUM PRIORITY TASKS

○ ☐

○ ☐

3 COULD DO TODAY
LIST THREE LOW PRIORITY TASKS

○ ☐

○ ☐

○ ☐

1 **MUST DO TODAY**
LIST ONE HIGH PRIORITY TASK

○ ☐

2 **SHOULD DO TODAY**
LIST TWO MEDIUM PRIORITY TASKS

○ ☐

○ ☐

3 **COULD DO TODAY**
LIST THREE LOW PRIORITY TASKS

○ ☐

○ ☐

○ ☐

1 **MUST DO TODAY**
LIST ONE HIGH PRIORITY TASK

○ ☐

2 **SHOULD DO TODAY**
LIST TWO MEDIUM PRIORITY TASKS

○ ☐

○ ☐

3 **COULD DO TODAY**
LIST THREE LOW PRIORITY TASKS

○ ☐

○ ☐

○ ☐

DATE_____

1 **MUST DO TODAY**
LIST ONE HIGH PRIORITY TASK

○ ☐

2 **SHOULD DO TODAY**
LIST TWO MEDIUM PRIORITY TASKS

○ ☐

○ ☐

3 **COULD DO TODAY**
LIST THREE LOW PRIORITY TASKS

○ ☐

○ ☐

○ ☐

1 MUST DO TODAY
LIST ONE HIGH PRIORITY TASK

2 SHOULD DO TODAY
LIST TWO MEDIUM PRIORITY TASKS

3 COULD DO TODAY
LIST THREE LOW PRIORITY TASKS

1 **MUST DO TODAY**
LIST ONE HIGH PRIORITY TASK

○ ☐

2 **SHOULD DO TODAY**
LIST TWO MEDIUM PRIORITY TASKS

○ ☐

○ ☐

3 **COULD DO TODAY**
LIST THREE LOW PRIORITY TASKS

○ ☐

○ ☐

○ ☐

1 **MUST DO TODAY**
LIST ONE HIGH PRIORITY TASK

○ ☐

2 **SHOULD DO TODAY**
LIST TWO MEDIUM PRIORITY TASKS

○ ☐

○ ☐

3 **COULD DO TODAY**
LIST THREE LOW PRIORITY TASKS

○ ☐

○ ☐

○ ☐

1 **MUST DO TODAY**
LIST ONE HIGH PRIORITY TASK

○ ☐

2 **SHOULD DO TODAY**
LIST TWO MEDIUM PRIORITY TASKS

○ ☐

○ ☐

3 **COULD DO TODAY**
LIST THREE LOW PRIORITY TASKS

○ ☐

○ ☐

○ ☐

DATE_____

1 **MUST DO TODAY**
LIST ONE HIGH PRIORITY TASK

2 **SHOULD DO TODAY**
LIST TWO MEDIUM PRIORITY TASKS

3 **COULD DO TODAY**
LIST THREE LOW PRIORITY TASKS

1 **MUST DO TODAY**
LIST ONE HIGH PRIORITY TASK

○

☐

2 **SHOULD DO TODAY**
LIST TWO MEDIUM PRIORITY TASKS

○

☐

○

☐

3 **COULD DO TODAY**
LIST THREE LOW PRIORITY TASKS

○ ☐

○ ☐

○ ☐

1 **MUST DO TODAY**
LIST ONE HIGH PRIORITY TASK

○ ☐

2 **SHOULD DO TODAY**
LIST TWO MEDIUM PRIORITY TASKS

○ ☐

○ ☐

3 **COULD DO TODAY**
LIST THREE LOW PRIORITY TASKS

○ ☐

○ ☐

○ ☐

DATE_____

1 MUST DO TODAY
LIST ONE HIGH PRIORITY TASK

○ ☐

2 SHOULD DO TODAY
LIST TWO MEDIUM PRIORITY TASKS

○ ☐

○ ☐

3 COULD DO TODAY
LIST THREE LOW PRIORITY TASKS

○ ☐

○ ☐

○ ☐

1 **MUST DO TODAY**
LIST ONE HIGH PRIORITY TASK

2 **SHOULD DO TODAY**
LIST TWO MEDIUM PRIORITY TASKS

3 **COULD DO TODAY**
LIST THREE LOW PRIORITY TASKS

1 **MUST DO TODAY**
LIST ONE HIGH PRIORITY TASK

○

2 **SHOULD DO TODAY**
LIST TWO MEDIUM PRIORITY TASKS

○

○

3 **COULD DO TODAY**
LIST THREE LOW PRIORITY TASKS

○

○

○

1 **MUST DO TODAY**
LIST ONE HIGH PRIORITY TASK

○ ☐

2 **SHOULD DO TODAY**
LIST TWO MEDIUM PRIORITY TASKS

○ ☐

○ ☐

3 **COULD DO TODAY**
LIST THREE LOW PRIORITY TASKS

○ ☐

○ ☐

○ ☐

1 **MUST DO TODAY**
LIST ONE HIGH PRIORITY TASK

○ ☐

2 **SHOULD DO TODAY**
LIST TWO MEDIUM PRIORITY TASKS

○ ☐

○ ☐

3 **COULD DO TODAY**
LIST THREE LOW PRIORITY TASKS

○ ☐

○ ☐

○ ☐

1 MUST DO TODAY
LIST ONE HIGH PRIORITY TASK

○ ☐

2 SHOULD DO TODAY
LIST TWO MEDIUM PRIORITY TASKS

○ ☐

○ ☐

3 COULD DO TODAY
LIST THREE LOW PRIORITY TASKS

○ ☐

○ ☐

○ ☐

DATE_____

1 **MUST DO TODAY**
LIST ONE HIGH PRIORITY TASK

○

2 **SHOULD DO TODAY**
LIST TWO MEDIUM PRIORITY TASKS

○

○

3 **COULD DO TODAY**
LIST THREE LOW PRIORITY TASKS

○

○

○

DATE_____

1 **MUST DO TODAY**
LIST ONE HIGH PRIORITY TASK

○

☐

2 **SHOULD DO TODAY**
LIST TWO MEDIUM PRIORITY TASKS

○

☐

○

☐

3 **COULD DO TODAY**
LIST THREE LOW PRIORITY TASKS

○ ☐

○ ☐

○ ☐

DATE_____

1 **MUST DO TODAY**
LIST ONE HIGH PRIORITY TASK

○

☐

2 **SHOULD DO TODAY**
LIST TWO MEDIUM PRIORITY TASKS

○

☐

○

☐

3 **COULD DO TODAY**
LIST THREE LOW PRIORITY TASKS

○   ☐

○   ☐

○   ☐

1 **MUST DO TODAY**
LIST ONE HIGH PRIORITY TASK

○ ☐

2 **SHOULD DO TODAY**
LIST TWO MEDIUM PRIORITY TASKS

○ ☐

○ ☐

3 **COULD DO TODAY**
LIST THREE LOW PRIORITY TASKS

○ ☐

○ ☐

○ ☐

1 **MUST DO TODAY**
LIST ONE HIGH PRIORITY TASK

○

☐

2 **SHOULD DO TODAY**
LIST TWO MEDIUM PRIORITY TASKS

○

☐

○

☐

3 **COULD DO TODAY**
LIST THREE LOW PRIORITY TASKS

○ ☐

○ ☐

○ ☐

1 **MUST DO TODAY**
LIST ONE HIGH PRIORITY TASK

○

2 **SHOULD DO TODAY**
LIST TWO MEDIUM PRIORITY TASKS

○

○

3 **COULD DO TODAY**
LIST THREE LOW PRIORITY TASKS

○

○

○

DATE_____

1 **MUST DO TODAY**
LIST ONE HIGH PRIORITY TASK

○ ☐

2 **SHOULD DO TODAY**
LIST TWO MEDIUM PRIORITY TASKS

○ ☐

○ ☐

3 **COULD DO TODAY**
LIST THREE LOW PRIORITY TASKS

○ ☐

○ ☐

○ ☐

1 **MUST DO TODAY**
LIST ONE HIGH PRIORITY TASK

○ ☐

2 **SHOULD DO TODAY**
LIST TWO MEDIUM PRIORITY TASKS

○ ☐

○ ☐

3 **COULD DO TODAY**
LIST THREE LOW PRIORITY TASKS

○ ☐

○ ☐

○ ☐

1 **MUST DO TODAY**
LIST ONE HIGH PRIORITY TASK

○
☐

2 **SHOULD DO TODAY**
LIST TWO MEDIUM PRIORITY TASKS

○
☐

○
☐

3 **COULD DO TODAY**
LIST THREE LOW PRIORITY TASKS

○
☐

○
☐

○
☐

1 MUST DO TODAY
LIST ONE HIGH PRIORITY TASK

○

2 SHOULD DO TODAY
LIST TWO MEDIUM PRIORITY TASKS

○

○

3 COULD DO TODAY
LIST THREE LOW PRIORITY TASKS

○

○

○

1 **MUST DO TODAY**
LIST ONE HIGH PRIORITY TASK

○

□

2 **SHOULD DO TODAY**
LIST TWO MEDIUM PRIORITY TASKS

○

□

○

□

3 **COULD DO TODAY**
LIST THREE LOW PRIORITY TASKS

○ □

○ □

○ □

1 MUST DO TODAY
LIST ONE HIGH PRIORITY TASK

○

☐

2 SHOULD DO TODAY
LIST TWO MEDIUM PRIORITY TASKS

○

☐

○

☐

3 COULD DO TODAY
LIST THREE LOW PRIORITY TASKS

○   ☐

○   ☐

○   ☐

1 **MUST DO TODAY**
LIST ONE HIGH PRIORITY TASK

○   ☐

2 **SHOULD DO TODAY**
LIST TWO MEDIUM PRIORITY TASKS

○   ☐

○   ☐

3 **COULD DO TODAY**
LIST THREE LOW PRIORITY TASKS

○   ☐

○   ☐

○   ☐

1 **MUST DO TODAY**
LIST ONE HIGH PRIORITY TASK

○   ☐

2 **SHOULD DO TODAY**
LIST TWO MEDIUM PRIORITY TASKS

○   ☐

○   ☐

3 **COULD DO TODAY**
LIST THREE LOW PRIORITY TASKS

○   ☐

○   ☐

○   ☐

1 MUST DO TODAY
LIST ONE HIGH PRIORITY TASK

○ ☐

2 SHOULD DO TODAY
LIST TWO MEDIUM PRIORITY TASKS

○ ☐

○ ☐

3 COULD DO TODAY
LIST THREE LOW PRIORITY TASKS

○ ☐

○ ☐

○ ☐

1 MUST DO TODAY
LIST ONE HIGH PRIORITY TASK

○

2 SHOULD DO TODAY
LIST TWO MEDIUM PRIORITY TASKS

○

○

3 COULD DO TODAY
LIST THREE LOW PRIORITY TASKS

○

○

○

1 MUST DO TODAY
LIST ONE HIGH PRIORITY TASK

○

☐

2 SHOULD DO TODAY
LIST TWO MEDIUM PRIORITY TASKS

○

☐

○

☐

3 COULD DO TODAY
LIST THREE LOW PRIORITY TASKS

○   ☐

○   ☐

○   ☐

DATE_____

1 **MUST DO TODAY**
LIST ONE HIGH PRIORITY TASK

○

☐

2 **SHOULD DO TODAY**
LIST TWO MEDIUM PRIORITY TASKS

○

☐

○

☐

3 **COULD DO TODAY**
LIST THREE LOW PRIORITY TASKS

○   ☐

○   ☐

○   ☐

1 **MUST DO TODAY**
LIST ONE HIGH PRIORITY TASK

○

☐

2 **SHOULD DO TODAY**
LIST TWO MEDIUM PRIORITY TASKS

○

☐

○

☐

3 **COULD DO TODAY**
LIST THREE LOW PRIORITY TASKS

○   ☐

○   ☐

○   ☐

DATE_____

1 MUST DO TODAY
LIST ONE HIGH PRIORITY TASK

○   ☐

2 SHOULD DO TODAY
LIST TWO MEDIUM PRIORITY TASKS

○   ☐

○   ☐

3 COULD DO TODAY
LIST THREE LOW PRIORITY TASKS

○   ☐

○   ☐

○   ☐

DATE_____

1 **MUST DO TODAY**
LIST ONE HIGH PRIORITY TASK

○ ☐

2 **SHOULD DO TODAY**
LIST TWO MEDIUM PRIORITY TASKS

○ ☐

○ ☐

3 **COULD DO TODAY**
LIST THREE LOW PRIORITY TASKS

○ ☐

○ ☐

○ ☐

1 **MUST DO TODAY**
LIST ONE HIGH PRIORITY TASK

○ ☐

2 **SHOULD DO TODAY**
LIST TWO MEDIUM PRIORITY TASKS

○ ☐

○ ☐

3 **COULD DO TODAY**
LIST THREE LOW PRIORITY TASKS

○ ☐

○ ☐

○ ☐

1 **MUST DO TODAY**
LIST ONE HIGH PRIORITY TASK

○

☐

2 **SHOULD DO TODAY**
LIST TWO MEDIUM PRIORITY TASKS

○

☐

○

☐

3 **COULD DO TODAY**
LIST THREE LOW PRIORITY TASKS

○   ☐

○   ☐

○   ☐

DATE_____

1 MUST DO TODAY
LIST ONE HIGH PRIORITY TASK

○

□

2 SHOULD DO TODAY
LIST TWO MEDIUM PRIORITY TASKS

○

□

○

□

3 COULD DO TODAY
LIST THREE LOW PRIORITY TASKS

○   □

○   □

○   □

1 MUST DO TODAY
LIST ONE HIGH PRIORITY TASK

○

☐

2 SHOULD DO TODAY
LIST TWO MEDIUM PRIORITY TASKS

○

☐

○

☐

3 COULD DO TODAY
LIST THREE LOW PRIORITY TASKS

○ ☐

○ ☐

○ ☐

1 **MUST DO TODAY**
LIST ONE HIGH PRIORITY TASK

○

☐

2 **SHOULD DO TODAY**
LIST TWO MEDIUM PRIORITY TASKS

○

☐

○

☐

3 **COULD DO TODAY**
LIST THREE LOW PRIORITY TASKS

○ ☐

○ ☐

○ ☐

1 MUST DO TODAY
LIST ONE HIGH PRIORITY TASK

○

☐

2 SHOULD DO TODAY
LIST TWO MEDIUM PRIORITY TASKS

○

☐

○

☐

3 COULD DO TODAY
LIST THREE LOW PRIORITY TASKS

○   ☐

○   ☐

○   ☐

1 **MUST DO TODAY**
LIST ONE HIGH PRIORITY TASK

○   ☐

2 **SHOULD DO TODAY**
LIST TWO MEDIUM PRIORITY TASKS

○   ☐

○   ☐

3 **COULD DO TODAY**
LIST THREE LOW PRIORITY TASKS

○   ☐

○   ☐

○   ☐

DATE_____

1 **MUST DO TODAY**
LIST ONE HIGH PRIORITY TASK

○

☐

2 **SHOULD DO TODAY**
LIST TWO MEDIUM PRIORITY TASKS

○

☐

○

☐

3 **COULD DO TODAY**
LIST THREE LOW PRIORITY TASKS

○   ☐

○   ☐

○   ☐

1 **MUST DO TODAY**
LIST ONE HIGH PRIORITY TASK

○ ▢

2 **SHOULD DO TODAY**
LIST TWO MEDIUM PRIORITY TASKS

○ ▢

○ ▢

3 **COULD DO TODAY**
LIST THREE LOW PRIORITY TASKS

○ ▢

○ ▢

○ ▢

DATE_____

1 **MUST DO TODAY**
LIST ONE HIGH PRIORITY TASK

○

2 **SHOULD DO TODAY**
LIST TWO MEDIUM PRIORITY TASKS

○

○

3 **COULD DO TODAY**
LIST THREE LOW PRIORITY TASKS

○

○

○

1 **MUST DO TODAY**
LIST ONE HIGH PRIORITY TASK

○

2 **SHOULD DO TODAY**
LIST TWO MEDIUM PRIORITY TASKS

○

○

3 **COULD DO TODAY**
LIST THREE LOW PRIORITY TASKS

○

○

○

DATE_____

1 **MUST DO TODAY**
LIST ONE HIGH PRIORITY TASK

○   ☐

2 **SHOULD DO TODAY**
LIST TWO MEDIUM PRIORITY TASKS

○   ☐

○   ☐

3 **COULD DO TODAY**
LIST THREE LOW PRIORITY TASKS

○   ☐

○   ☐

○   ☐

1 **MUST DO TODAY**
LIST ONE HIGH PRIORITY TASK

○

2 **SHOULD DO TODAY**
LIST TWO MEDIUM PRIORITY TASKS

○

○

3 **COULD DO TODAY**
LIST THREE LOW PRIORITY TASKS

○

○

○

DATE_____

1 **MUST DO TODAY**
LIST ONE HIGH PRIORITY TASK

○   ☐

2 **SHOULD DO TODAY**
LIST TWO MEDIUM PRIORITY TASKS

○   ☐

○   ☐

3 **COULD DO TODAY**
LIST THREE LOW PRIORITY TASKS

○   ☐

○   ☐

○   ☐

1 **MUST DO TODAY**
LIST ONE HIGH PRIORITY TASK

○ ☐

2 **SHOULD DO TODAY**
LIST TWO MEDIUM PRIORITY TASKS

○ ☐

○ ☐

3 **COULD DO TODAY**
LIST THREE LOW PRIORITY TASKS

○ ☐

○ ☐

○ ☐

1 **MUST DO TODAY**
LIST ONE HIGH PRIORITY TASK

○

☐

2 **SHOULD DO TODAY**
LIST TWO MEDIUM PRIORITY TASKS

○

☐

○

☐

3 **COULD DO TODAY**
LIST THREE LOW PRIORITY TASKS

○   ☐

○   ☐

○   ☐

1 **MUST DO TODAY**
LIST ONE HIGH PRIORITY TASK

○ ☐

2 **SHOULD DO TODAY**
LIST TWO MEDIUM PRIORITY TASKS

○ ☐

○ ☐

3 **COULD DO TODAY**
LIST THREE LOW PRIORITY TASKS

○ ☐

○ ☐

○ ☐

DATE_____

1 **MUST DO TODAY**
LIST ONE HIGH PRIORITY TASK

○   ☐

2 **SHOULD DO TODAY**
LIST TWO MEDIUM PRIORITY TASKS

○   ☐

○   ☐

3 **COULD DO TODAY**
LIST THREE LOW PRIORITY TASKS

○   ☐

○   ☐

○   ☐

1 **MUST DO TODAY**
LIST ONE HIGH PRIORITY TASK

○ ☐

2 **SHOULD DO TODAY**
LIST TWO MEDIUM PRIORITY TASKS

○ ☐

○ ☐

3 **COULD DO TODAY**
LIST THREE LOW PRIORITY TASKS

○ ☐

○ ☐

○ ☐

1 MUST DO TODAY
LIST ONE HIGH PRIORITY TASK

○ ☐

2 SHOULD DO TODAY
LIST TWO MEDIUM PRIORITY TASKS

○ ☐

○ ☐

3 COULD DO TODAY
LIST THREE LOW PRIORITY TASKS

○ ☐

○ ☐

○ ☐

1 **MUST DO TODAY**
LIST ONE HIGH PRIORITY TASK

2 **SHOULD DO TODAY**
LIST TWO MEDIUM PRIORITY TASKS

3 **COULD DO TODAY**
LIST THREE LOW PRIORITY TASKS

1 **MUST DO TODAY**
LIST ONE HIGH PRIORITY TASK

○

☐

2 **SHOULD DO TODAY**
LIST TWO MEDIUM PRIORITY TASKS

○

☐

○

☐

3 **COULD DO TODAY**
LIST THREE LOW PRIORITY TASKS

○   ☐

○   ☐

○   ☐

1 **MUST DO TODAY**
LIST ONE HIGH PRIORITY TASK

○   ☐

2 **SHOULD DO TODAY**
LIST TWO MEDIUM PRIORITY TASKS

○   ☐

○   ☐

3 **COULD DO TODAY**
LIST THREE LOW PRIORITY TASKS

○   ☐

○   ☐

○   ☐

1 **MUST DO TODAY**
LIST ONE HIGH PRIORITY TASK

○   ☐

2 **SHOULD DO TODAY**
LIST TWO MEDIUM PRIORITY TASKS

○   ☐

○   ☐

3 **COULD DO TODAY**
LIST THREE LOW PRIORITY TASKS

○   ☐

○   ☐

○   ☐

1 **MUST DO TODAY**
LIST ONE HIGH PRIORITY TASK

○ ☐

2 **SHOULD DO TODAY**
LIST TWO MEDIUM PRIORITY TASKS

○ ☐

○ ☐

3 **COULD DO TODAY**
LIST THREE LOW PRIORITY TASKS

○ ☐

○ ☐

○ ☐

1 **MUST DO TODAY**
LIST ONE HIGH PRIORITY TASK

○ ☐

2 **SHOULD DO TODAY**
LIST TWO MEDIUM PRIORITY TASKS

○ ☐

○ ☐

3 **COULD DO TODAY**
LIST THREE LOW PRIORITY TASKS

○ ☐

○ ☐

○ ☐

1 **MUST DO TODAY**
LIST ONE HIGH PRIORITY TASK

○

□

2 **SHOULD DO TODAY**
LIST TWO MEDIUM PRIORITY TASKS

○

□

○

□

3 **COULD DO TODAY**
LIST THREE LOW PRIORITY TASKS

○

□

○

□

○

□

DATE_____

1 **MUST DO TODAY**
LIST ONE HIGH PRIORITY TASK

○ ☐

2 **SHOULD DO TODAY**
LIST TWO MEDIUM PRIORITY TASKS

○ ☐

○ ☐

3 **COULD DO TODAY**
LIST THREE LOW PRIORITY TASKS

○ ☐

○ ☐

○ ☐

1 **MUST DO TODAY**
LIST ONE HIGH PRIORITY TASK

○ ☐

2 **SHOULD DO TODAY**
LIST TWO MEDIUM PRIORITY TASKS

○ ☐

○ ☐

3 **COULD DO TODAY**
LIST THREE LOW PRIORITY TASKS

○ ☐

○ ☐

○ ☐

DATE_____

1 **MUST DO TODAY**
LIST ONE HIGH PRIORITY TASK

○ ☐

2 **SHOULD DO TODAY**
LIST TWO MEDIUM PRIORITY TASKS

○ ☐

○ ☐

3 **COULD DO TODAY**
LIST THREE LOW PRIORITY TASKS

○ ☐

○ ☐

○ ☐

1 **MUST DO TODAY**
LIST ONE HIGH PRIORITY TASK

○ ☐

2 **SHOULD DO TODAY**
LIST TWO MEDIUM PRIORITY TASKS

○ ☐

○ ☐

3 **COULD DO TODAY**
LIST THREE LOW PRIORITY TASKS

○ ☐

○ ☐

○ ☐

1 **MUST DO TODAY**
LIST ONE HIGH PRIORITY TASK

○ ☐

2 **SHOULD DO TODAY**
LIST TWO MEDIUM PRIORITY TASKS

○ ☐

○ ☐

3 **COULD DO TODAY**
LIST THREE LOW PRIORITY TASKS

○ ☐

○ ☐

○ ☐

1 **MUST DO TODAY**
LIST ONE HIGH PRIORITY TASK

○ ☐

2 **SHOULD DO TODAY**
LIST TWO MEDIUM PRIORITY TASKS

○ ☐

○ ☐

3 **COULD DO TODAY**
LIST THREE LOW PRIORITY TASKS

○ ☐

○ ☐

○ ☐

1 **MUST DO TODAY**
LIST ONE HIGH PRIORITY TASK

○
☐

2 **SHOULD DO TODAY**
LIST TWO MEDIUM PRIORITY TASKS

○
☐

○
☐

3 **COULD DO TODAY**
LIST THREE LOW PRIORITY TASKS

○ ☐

○ ☐

○ ☐

1 MUST DO TODAY
LIST ONE HIGH PRIORITY TASK

○ ☐

2 SHOULD DO TODAY
LIST TWO MEDIUM PRIORITY TASKS

○ ☐

○ ☐

3 COULD DO TODAY
LIST THREE LOW PRIORITY TASKS

○ ☐

○ ☐

○ ☐

1 **MUST DO TODAY**
LIST ONE HIGH PRIORITY TASK

○

☐

2 **SHOULD DO TODAY**
LIST TWO MEDIUM PRIORITY TASKS

○

☐

○

☐

3 **COULD DO TODAY**
LIST THREE LOW PRIORITY TASKS

○ ☐

○ ☐

○ ☐

1 MUST DO TODAY
LIST ONE HIGH PRIORITY TASK

○ ☐

2 SHOULD DO TODAY
LIST TWO MEDIUM PRIORITY TASKS

○ ☐

○ ☐

3 COULD DO TODAY
LIST THREE LOW PRIORITY TASKS

○ ☐

○ ☐

○ ☐

1 MUST DO TODAY
LIST ONE HIGH PRIORITY TASK

○

2 SHOULD DO TODAY
LIST TWO MEDIUM PRIORITY TASKS

○

○

3 COULD DO TODAY
LIST THREE LOW PRIORITY TASKS

○

○

○

DATE_____

1 **MUST DO TODAY**
LIST ONE HIGH PRIORITY TASK

○ ☐

2 **SHOULD DO TODAY**
LIST TWO MEDIUM PRIORITY TASKS

○ ☐

○ ☐

3 **COULD DO TODAY**
LIST THREE LOW PRIORITY TASKS

○ ☐

○ ☐

○ ☐

DATE_____

1 **MUST DO TODAY**
LIST ONE HIGH PRIORITY TASK

○

☐

2 **SHOULD DO TODAY**
LIST TWO MEDIUM PRIORITY TASKS

○

☐

○

☐

3 **COULD DO TODAY**
LIST THREE LOW PRIORITY TASKS

○   ☐

○   ☐

○   ☐

1 **MUST DO TODAY**
LIST ONE HIGH PRIORITY TASK

○ ☐

2 **SHOULD DO TODAY**
LIST TWO MEDIUM PRIORITY TASKS

○ ☐

○ ☐

3 **COULD DO TODAY**
LIST THREE LOW PRIORITY TASKS

○ ☐

○ ☐

○ ☐

1 MUST DO TODAY
LIST ONE HIGH PRIORITY TASK

○

☐

2 SHOULD DO TODAY
LIST TWO MEDIUM PRIORITY TASKS

○

☐

○

☐

3 COULD DO TODAY
LIST THREE LOW PRIORITY TASKS

○ ☐

○ ☐

○ ☐

1 **MUST DO TODAY**
LIST ONE HIGH PRIORITY TASK

2 **SHOULD DO TODAY**
LIST TWO MEDIUM PRIORITY TASKS

3 **COULD DO TODAY**
LIST THREE LOW PRIORITY TASKS

1 **MUST DO TODAY**
LIST ONE HIGH PRIORITY TASK

○ ☐

2 **SHOULD DO TODAY**
LIST TWO MEDIUM PRIORITY TASKS

○ ☐

○ ☐

3 **COULD DO TODAY**
LIST THREE LOW PRIORITY TASKS

○ ☐

○ ☐

○ ☐

DATE_____

1 **MUST DO TODAY**
LIST ONE HIGH PRIORITY TASK

○ ☐

2 **SHOULD DO TODAY**
LIST TWO MEDIUM PRIORITY TASKS

○ ☐

○ ☐

3 **COULD DO TODAY**
LIST THREE LOW PRIORITY TASKS

○ ☐

○ ☐

○ ☐

1 **MUST DO TODAY**
LIST ONE HIGH PRIORITY TASK

○   ☐

2 **SHOULD DO TODAY**
LIST TWO MEDIUM PRIORITY TASKS

○   ☐

○   ☐

3 **COULD DO TODAY**
LIST THREE LOW PRIORITY TASKS

○   ☐

○   ☐

○   ☐

1 **MUST DO TODAY**
LIST ONE HIGH PRIORITY TASK

○ ☐

2 **SHOULD DO TODAY**
LIST TWO MEDIUM PRIORITY TASKS

○ ☐

○ ☐

3 **COULD DO TODAY**
LIST THREE LOW PRIORITY TASKS

○ ☐

○ ☐

○ ☐

1 **MUST DO TODAY**
LIST ONE HIGH PRIORITY TASK

○

2 **SHOULD DO TODAY**
LIST TWO MEDIUM PRIORITY TASKS

○

○

3 **COULD DO TODAY**
LIST THREE LOW PRIORITY TASKS

○

○

○

DATE_____

1 **MUST DO TODAY**
LIST ONE HIGH PRIORITY TASK

○
☐

2 **SHOULD DO TODAY**
LIST TWO MEDIUM PRIORITY TASKS

○
☐

○
☐

3 **COULD DO TODAY**
LIST THREE LOW PRIORITY TASKS

○
☐

○
☐

○
☐

1 MUST DO TODAY
LIST ONE HIGH PRIORITY TASK

○   ☐

2 SHOULD DO TODAY
LIST TWO MEDIUM PRIORITY TASKS

○   ☐

○   ☐

3 COULD DO TODAY
LIST THREE LOW PRIORITY TASKS

○   ☐

○   ☐

○   ☐

1 MUST DO TODAY
LIST ONE HIGH PRIORITY TASK

○ ☐

2 SHOULD DO TODAY
LIST TWO MEDIUM PRIORITY TASKS

○ ☐

○ ☐

3 COULD DO TODAY
LIST THREE LOW PRIORITY TASKS

○ ☐

○ ☐

○ ☐

1 MUST DO TODAY
LIST ONE HIGH PRIORITY TASK

○ ☐

2 SHOULD DO TODAY
LIST TWO MEDIUM PRIORITY TASKS

○ ☐

○ ☐

3 COULD DO TODAY
LIST THREE LOW PRIORITY TASKS

○ ☐

○ ☐

○ ☐

1 **MUST DO TODAY**
LIST ONE HIGH PRIORITY TASK

2 **SHOULD DO TODAY**
LIST TWO MEDIUM PRIORITY TASKS

3 **COULD DO TODAY**
LIST THREE LOW PRIORITY TASKS

1 MUST DO TODAY
LIST ONE HIGH PRIORITY TASK

○ ☐

2 SHOULD DO TODAY
LIST TWO MEDIUM PRIORITY TASKS

○ ☐

○ ☐

3 COULD DO TODAY
LIST THREE LOW PRIORITY TASKS

○ ☐

○ ☐

○ ☐

DATE_____

1 **MUST DO TODAY**
LIST ONE HIGH PRIORITY TASK

○

☐

2 **SHOULD DO TODAY**
LIST TWO MEDIUM PRIORITY TASKS

○

☐

○

☐

3 **COULD DO TODAY**
LIST THREE LOW PRIORITY TASKS

○ ☐

○ ☐

○ ☐

1 **MUST DO TODAY**
LIST ONE HIGH PRIORITY TASK

○

☐

2 **SHOULD DO TODAY**
LIST TWO MEDIUM PRIORITY TASKS

○

☐

○

☐

3 **COULD DO TODAY**
LIST THREE LOW PRIORITY TASKS

○ ☐

○ ☐

○ ☐

1 **MUST DO TODAY**
LIST ONE HIGH PRIORITY TASK

○ ☐

2 **SHOULD DO TODAY**
LIST TWO MEDIUM PRIORITY TASKS

○ ☐

○ ☐

3 **COULD DO TODAY**
LIST THREE LOW PRIORITY TASKS

○ ☐

○ ☐

○ ☐

1 **MUST DO TODAY**
LIST ONE HIGH PRIORITY TASK

○

☐

2 **SHOULD DO TODAY**
LIST TWO MEDIUM PRIORITY TASKS

○

☐

○

☐

3 **COULD DO TODAY**
LIST THREE LOW PRIORITY TASKS

○ ☐

○ ☐

○ ☐

1 MUST DO TODAY
LIST ONE HIGH PRIORITY TASK

○ ☐

2 SHOULD DO TODAY
LIST TWO MEDIUM PRIORITY TASKS

○ ☐

○ ☐

3 COULD DO TODAY
LIST THREE LOW PRIORITY TASKS

○ ☐

○ ☐

○ ☐

1 MUST DO TODAY
LIST ONE HIGH PRIORITY TASK

○

☐

2 SHOULD DO TODAY
LIST TWO MEDIUM PRIORITY TASKS

○

☐

○

☐

3 COULD DO TODAY
LIST THREE LOW PRIORITY TASKS

○ ☐

○ ☐

○ ☐

1 **MUST DO TODAY**
LIST ONE HIGH PRIORITY TASK

○

2 **SHOULD DO TODAY**
LIST TWO MEDIUM PRIORITY TASKS

○

○

3 **COULD DO TODAY**
LIST THREE LOW PRIORITY TASKS

○

○

○

1 **MUST DO TODAY**
LIST ONE HIGH PRIORITY TASK

2 **SHOULD DO TODAY**
LIST TWO MEDIUM PRIORITY TASKS

3 **COULD DO TODAY**
LIST THREE LOW PRIORITY TASKS

1 **MUST DO TODAY**
LIST ONE HIGH PRIORITY TASK

○

2 **SHOULD DO TODAY**
LIST TWO MEDIUM PRIORITY TASKS

○

○

3 **COULD DO TODAY**
LIST THREE LOW PRIORITY TASKS

○

○

○

1 MUST DO TODAY
LIST ONE HIGH PRIORITY TASK

○

☐

2 SHOULD DO TODAY
LIST TWO MEDIUM PRIORITY TASKS

○

☐

○

☐

3 COULD DO TODAY
LIST THREE LOW PRIORITY TASKS

○ ☐

○ ☐

○ ☐

1 **MUST DO TODAY**
LIST ONE HIGH PRIORITY TASK

○ ☐

2 **SHOULD DO TODAY**
LIST TWO MEDIUM PRIORITY TASKS

○ ☐

○ ☐

3 **COULD DO TODAY**
LIST THREE LOW PRIORITY TASKS

○ ☐

○ ☐

○ ☐

1 **MUST DO TODAY**
LIST ONE HIGH PRIORITY TASK

○

☐

2 **SHOULD DO TODAY**
LIST TWO MEDIUM PRIORITY TASKS

○

☐

○

☐

3 **COULD DO TODAY**
LIST THREE LOW PRIORITY TASKS

○   ☐

○   ☐

○   ☐

DATE_____

1 **MUST DO TODAY**
LIST ONE HIGH PRIORITY TASK

○ ☐

2 **SHOULD DO TODAY**
LIST TWO MEDIUM PRIORITY TASKS

○ ☐

○ ☐

3 **COULD DO TODAY**
LIST THREE LOW PRIORITY TASKS

○ ☐

○ ☐

○ ☐

1 **MUST DO TODAY**
LIST ONE HIGH PRIORITY TASK

○ ☐

2 **SHOULD DO TODAY**
LIST TWO MEDIUM PRIORITY TASKS

○ ☐

○ ☐

3 **COULD DO TODAY**
LIST THREE LOW PRIORITY TASKS

○ ☐

○ ☐

○ ☐

1 **MUST DO TODAY**
LIST ONE HIGH PRIORITY TASK

2 **SHOULD DO TODAY**
LIST TWO MEDIUM PRIORITY TASKS

3 **COULD DO TODAY**
LIST THREE LOW PRIORITY TASKS

DATE_____

1 **MUST DO TODAY**
LIST ONE HIGH PRIORITY TASK

○

☐

2 **SHOULD DO TODAY**
LIST TWO MEDIUM PRIORITY TASKS

○

☐

○

☐

3 **COULD DO TODAY**
LIST THREE LOW PRIORITY TASKS

○   ☐

○   ☐

○   ☐

NOTES / SCHEDULE / OTHER

New ideas, inspiration, goals, appointments, contacts, observations, etc.

_____

_____

_____

_____

_____

_____

_____

_____

_____

_____

_____

_____

_____

_____

_____

NOTES / SCHEDULE / OTHER

New ideas, inspiration, goals, appointments, contacts, observations, etc.

_____

_____

_____

_____

_____

_____

_____

_____

_____

_____

_____

_____

_____

_____

_____

_____

_____

NOTES / SCHEDULE / OTHER

New ideas, inspiration, goals, appointments, contacts, observations, etc.

NOTES / SCHEDULE / OTHER

New ideas, inspiration, goals, appointments, contacts, observations, etc.

NOTES / SCHEDULE / OTHER

New ideas, inspiration, goals, appointments, contacts, observations, etc.

NOTES / SCHEDULE / OTHER

New ideas, inspiration, goals, appointments, contacts, observations, etc.

NOTES / SCHEDULE / OTHER

New ideas, inspiration, goals, appointments, contacts, observations, etc.

NOTES / SCHEDULE / OTHER

New ideas, inspiration, goals, appointments, contacts, observations, etc.

NOTES / SCHEDULE / OTHER

New ideas, inspiration, goals, appointments, contacts, observations, etc.

NOTES / SCHEDULE / OTHER

New ideas, inspiration, goals, appointments, contacts, observations, etc.

IF FOUND, PLEASE CONTACT:

_____

_____